p. 1 Check?

MW01107811

# CONTEMPORARY ACOUSTIC GUITAR SKILLS

## FOR MUSIC LEADERS

### 15 Totally Hip Techniques for Therapy, Education, Recreation and Leisure

## ROBERT KROUT
### ED.D., RMT-BC

**MMB**

MMB MUSIC, INC.

# CONTEMPORARY ACOUSTIC GUITAR SKILLS FOR MUSIC LEADERS

*15 Totally Hip Techniques for Therapy, Education, Recreation and Leisure*
Robert Krout, Ed.D., RMT-BC

© Copyright 1995 MMB Music, Inc. All rights reserved. International protection secured under Berne, UCC, Buenos Aires and bilateral copyright treaties. No part of this publication may be reproduced, stored in a retrieval system, or transmitted—in any form or by any means now known or later developed—without prior written permission except in the case of brief quotations embodied in critical articles and reviews.

Cover design: Michael Kilfoy, Studio X, St. Louis, Missouri
Music Engraver & Typographer: MusicScribe, Columbia, South Carolina
Editor: Carl Simpson
Printer: Schaum PressWorks, Mequon, Wisconsin
First printing: May, 1996
Printed in USA
ISBN: 0-918812-86-0

For further information and catalogs, contact:

MMB Music, Inc.
Contemporary Arts Building
3526 Washington Avenue
Saint Louis, MO 63103-1019

Phone: 314 531-9635; 800 543-3771 (USA/Canada)
Fax:     314 531-8384

# Table of Contents

# About This Book: My Goals for You and Your Clients/Students

The acoustic guitar is used by music leaders in many settings. These include: clinical music therapy sessions, music education classes, individual and group music lessons, summer camps, after-school recreation settings, community group homes for persons with developmental and mental challenges, etc. Acoustic guitar may be used by the music leader as an accompaniment instrument for singing, creating and composing music, movement, or listening. In addition, guitar instruction can provide an environment for behavioral change through music experiences.

While many music leaders play some folk guitar, most have not had training in contemporary acoustic guitar skills. By contemporary, I mean techniques that are beyond the scope of most beginning guitar classes offered at colleges and universities where these leaders are trained. The guitar training of music leaders usually consists of one or two semesters of basic folk and/or classical technique. These skills are best suited to playing songs which use open or barre chords, straight forward strums or arpeggio patterns, simple left-hand techniques, such as hammer-ons and pull-offs, some bass runs, and the like. However, the reality is, music leaders are often required to play and teach guitar in styles that have evolved since the explosion of rock music in the 1960s. These skills are usually beyond the scope of college guitar classes.

The acoustic guitar has been used in popular songs from Buddy (Holly) to the Beatles to the Black Crowes, and the 1990s have seen a tremendous surge of interest in acoustic guitar music and playing. The phenomenally successful Unplugged series on MTV has brought the acoustic renderings of groups ranging from Nirvana to Neil Young into homes and education/health/leisure facilities across the country. As a result, our music consumer groups (including students, clients, residents, campers and patients) request songs played on acoustic guitar. Music leaders, thus, must be able to play, teach, and utilize acoustic guitar skills that sound authentic and are motivating to these consumer groups.

My goals for this book are simple and straightforward; they all involve having you and your clients/students playing interesting acoustic guitar while ensuring success along the sometimes rocky road of learning. Whether you are a music therapist, music educator, recreation leader, church guitarist, or anyone else interested in improving your acoustic playing, you are welcome here! The overall goals I have include:

1. For you to become a better guitarist yourself.
2. For you to help improve the guitar playing of those with whom you work.
3. For you to be successful during the process of learning new skills.
4. For you to ensure the success of your clients during their process of learning.
5. For you and your clients/students to learn skills which can transfer (generalize) to many forms of contemporary music.

# Overview of Skill Learning, Use and Teaching, including forms from *Beginning Rock Guitar for Music Leaders*

In order for music leaders to be proficient in post 1960s acoustic guitar techniques, new curricular materials are needed. This book outlines a core of essential skills and presents them in a tested and proven method for two major application areas. First, the book will help music leaders themselves learn and become proficient at these skills. While the book will not replace a teacher, it can be used by the music leader who has some folk guitar experience. A teacher is always recommended for the leader learning these skills. Second, the book will be useful to music leaders (especially music therapists) who use guitar instruction as a part of their work. This is because the skills are broken down into subskills, or smaller units, for teaching. Thus, it will be easier for leaders and therapists to help their students/clients learn the skills bit by bit over time.

This book is the third in a guitar series. *Teaching Basic Guitar Skills to Special Learners* (MMB Music, 1983, revised second edition 1986) and *Beginning Rock Guitar for Music Leaders* (MMB Music, 1994) are the previous titles. These books detail instruction and teaching methods geared to working with learners with special needs. I recommend that you start by reading chapters one and two of *Beginning Rock Guitar for Music Leaders* to become familiar with suggestion on topics including: an overview of teaching techniques, modeling and prompting, the use of visual aids, charts, tablature, breaking down skills into subskills, teaching outlines, the use of songs for teaching vehicles, teaching arrangements (1:1, 1:2, and groups), using this book series with groups of students, graphing progress, assessing your students' skill levels, and assessing student music preferences. Many of the skills contained in the above book may also be adapted for and played on acoustic guitar. You may wish to combine aspects of both books in your playing and teaching.

The fifteen skills will be presented in the form of teaching outlines. Each outline contains information relating to fingering chords and progressions, playing strums, picks and plucks, and other information. Each skill is broken down into smaller subskills for easier learning. The subskills are numbered from 1 to 4, with 1 being the easiest and subskills 2, 3, and 4 being progressively more difficult. The idea is to start with the easiest subskill and gradually add the more difficult aspects of the skill until the final target skill is learned. This is a simplified use of one variant of the task analysis approach. It is also known as shaping, because you are starting from the student's (or your) level and gradually moving toward the final target. Skills are presented in chord chart form, in tablature, and the notes involved are also represented on a treble staff (although not in the note order of the strings played). A data collection area is located at the bottom of each teaching outline, along with a prompt code. With this information, you can keep track of learning over time. You may wish to graph this progress to share with teachers, parents, the student, the treatment team, and anyone else interested in the progress of the student. Remember to read the corresponding information from *Beginning Rock Guitar for Music Leaders* for a review of how the teaching and graphing process works.

This book will begin with an overview of the acoustic guitar skills to be covered, and we will then get right down to learning and playing an exciting array of beginning contemporary acoustic guitar skills that will (hopefully) change your playing forever! I would like to stress that this book is not intended to be a comprehensive acoustic guitar method. It is designed to get you and your consumers off to the right start in learning these contemporary skills. By breaking skills down into smaller and easier-to-learn units, you can experience success while developing your technique. In the future, you can adapt this skill-analysis process to many other guitar skills found in magazines and books.

# A Note for Left-Handed Learners

It is not uncommon for the music leader to encounter a learner who is left-hand dominant, or left-handed. You may be left-handed yourself. There are several possibilities which you may consider in deciding how to present the skills.

1. Learn and play the skills as written, with the left hand fingering chords and the right hand strumming. Many left-handed learners report little difficulty doing this. They have often learned in this manner simply because a left-handed guitar was not available to them when they were beginning.

2. Turn the guitar upside down and play it with the right hand now fingering the chords. This may not be possible, due to the shape of the guitar. Asymmetric guitars often have much smaller treble-side horns and/or shoulders. This technique also places the bass strings away from the learner, making chord fingering essentially an upside down process (the chord charts will now be upside down as well).

3. If the upside-down guitar (with neck pointing to the right from the vantage point of the learner) fits on the lap or can be played comfortably with a strap, you might consider changing strings so that the bass strings once again are closest to the learner. If you do this, use extra light gauge or electric guitar strings. Guitars are designed to have the maximum string tension on the traditional bass side, and have bracing under the wood to accommodate this substantial tension and pull. Using heavier strings might cause the top of the guitar to twist and pull.

4. Get hold of a left-handed guitar. They are not common, and may have to be ordered, although a good music store will usually have a few in stock.

Our overriding principle is the success of the learner. Choose the route that you believe will allow the learner the greatest success in the long run. Remember that guitar books represent chord charts in right-hand form. This book does the same, and I assume throughout that you and your learners are fingering with the left hand and strumming with the right. If this is not the case (I apologize for discriminating against you left-handed guitarists), be sure to reverse hands on skills that specify a hand to be used (e.g. "Rhythmic Strum with Right-Hand Damping" would really be "…with Left-Hand Damping"). Good Luck!

# Teaching Outline for Chords

Student _____

Skill# _____ Skill Description

Subskills  I. _____
         II. _____
       III. _____
       IV. _____

## PROGRESS DATA

| Date | | | | | | | | | | | |
|---|---|---|---|---|---|---|---|---|---|---|---|
| Subskill #(s) | | | | | | | | | | | |
| Prompt Level | | | | | | | | | | | |

| Date | | | | | | | | | | | |
|---|---|---|---|---|---|---|---|---|---|---|---|
| Subskill #(s) | | | | | | | | | | | |
| Prompt Level | | | | | | | | | | | |

Prompts:     **I**–Independent;  **G**–Gestural;  **P**–Physical;  **M**–Manipulative;  **O**–Subskill/Skill not performed.

# Teaching Outline for Strums/Leads/Progressions

Student _____

Skill# _____ Skill Description

Subskills  I. _____

          II. _____

        III. _____

        IV. _____

Skill Notation                              Strum

## PROGRESS DATA

| Date | | | | | | | | | | | | | |
|---|---|---|---|---|---|---|---|---|---|---|---|---|---|
| Subskill #(s) | | | | | | | | | | | | | |
| Prompt Level | | | | | | | | | | | | | |

| Date | | | | | | | | | | | | | |
|---|---|---|---|---|---|---|---|---|---|---|---|---|---|
| Subskill #(s) | | | | | | | | | | | | | |
| Prompt Level | | | | | | | | | | | | | |

Prompts:     **I**−Independent; **G**−Gestural; **P**−Physical; **M**−Manipulative; **O**−Subskill/Skill not performed.

# Teaching Outline Graph

from: Krout, R.: *Teaching Basic Guitar Skills to Special Learners.* St. Louis: MMB Music, Inc. (1983)

Student _____ Teacher _____ Lesson Time _____

Objective _____

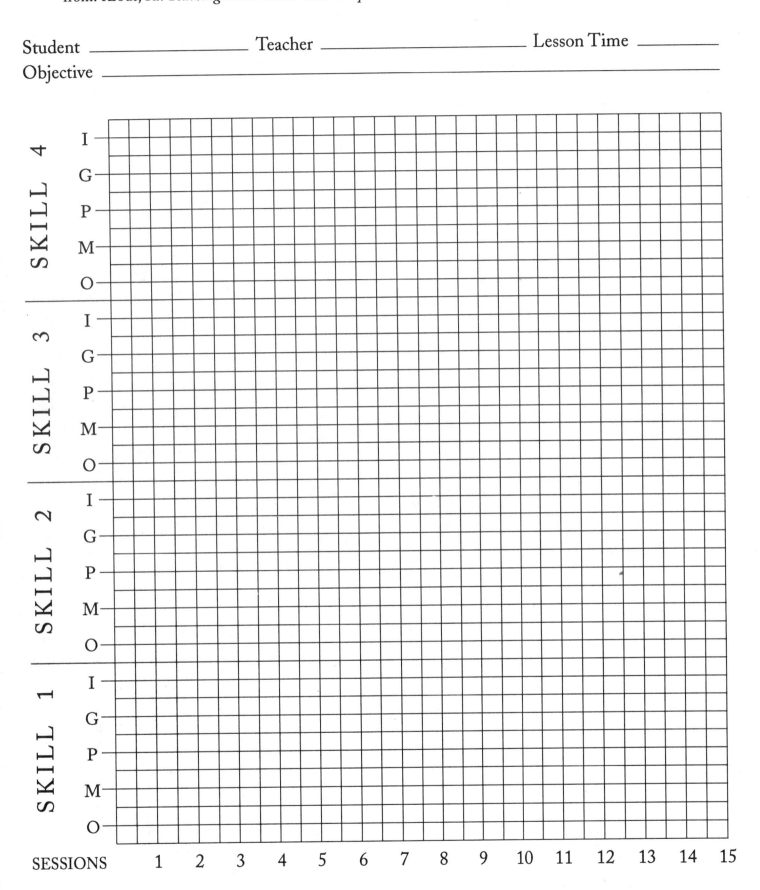

© Copyright 1983 MMB Music, Inc. St. Louis, MO USA

All rights reserved. International Teaching protection secured under UCC, Buenos Aires and bilateral copyright treaties. No part of this publication may be reproduced, stored in a retrieval system, or transmitted in any form or by any means now known or later developed without the prior written permission of the copyright owner.

# Teaching Outline Graph

from: Krout, R.: *Teaching Basic Guitar Skills to Special Learners*. St. Louis: MMB Music, Inc. (1983)

Student _____ Teacher _____ Lesson Time _____

Objective _____

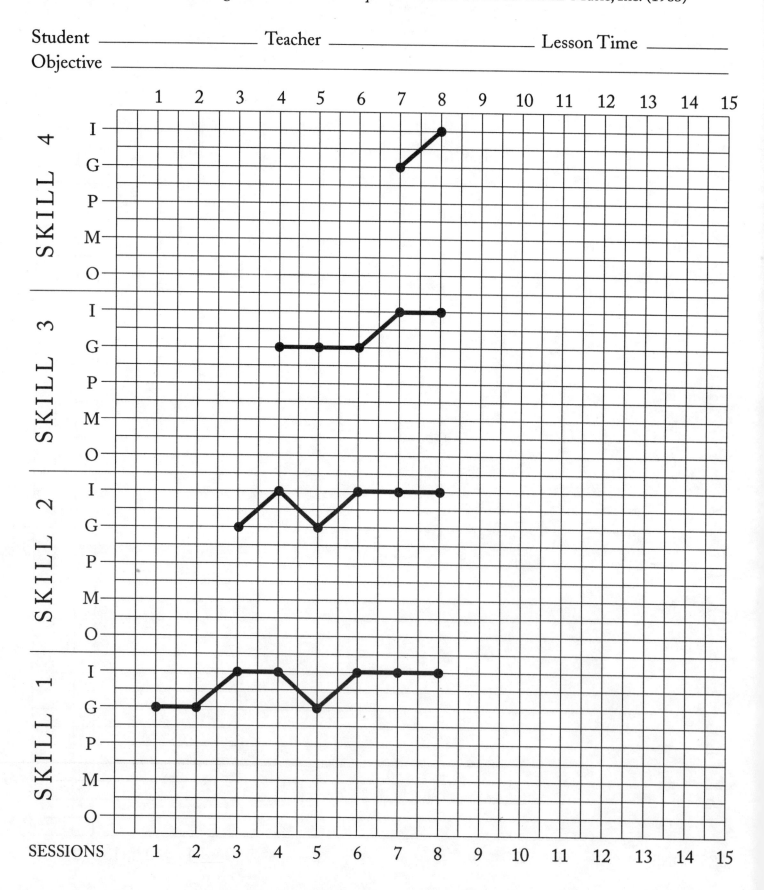

© Copyright 1983 MMB Music, Inc. St. Louis, MO USA

All rights reserved. International protection secured under UCC, Buenos Aires and bilateral copyright treaties. No part of this publication may be reproduced, stored in a retrieval system, or transmitted in any form or by any means now known or later developed without the prior written permission of the copyright owner.

# FIFTEEN CONTEMPORARY ACOUSTIC GUITAR SKILLS

# Fifteen Contemporary Acoustic Guitar Skills

## HOW SKILLS WERE CHOSEN

The fifteen skills presented in this book represent a sample of the thousands of possibilities available for your acoustic use. I have selected what I feel is a sampling of various techniques I enjoy using in my playing and that are representative of contemporary acoustic possibilities. The skills are also designed to get your fingers used to moving and behaving in new ways. It is hoped that this book will be just the beginning for you and your students. Once you have mastered these, apply your new abilities to learn skills and songs presented in the hundreds of more advanced guitar methods, magazines, videos, and of course songs that use acoustic guitar. In addition, look for future volumes in the MMB special guitar series which will cover additional topics and skill areas such as blues, altered tunings, jazz, and more.

## SKILLS #1–11: ACTIVE CHORDS, PATTERNS, AND PROGRESSIONS

Chords are the bread and butter of acoustic guitar playing. While some acoustic players may play only leads (as the rhythm guitarist strums away in the background) many of today's finest guitarists play chord-based progressions as well as leads in their songs. These include contemporary players such as Nuno Bettencourt, Paul Gilbert, Eric Johnson, Richie Sambora and others. Chords and progressions allow us to set tonality and tonal movement for singing, moving, improvising, writing songs and other guitar-based activities. While you may already play chords on your acoustic, you probably use mostly static open-position, power, or barre chords. By static I mean that you keep the same chord position going unchanged until you switch to a new chord. The following chord skills are designed to be active, or moving within a key or chord function (such as tonic, dominant seventh, etc.) For instance, if you currently were to see four measures of a G chord in a song, you probably stay on an open position G and only move your fingers when it is time for the next chord (maybe throwing in a bass run to connect to the new chord). We will call this a static approach. An active approach might be to play a vamp centered around, but not only using a G chord. You could substitute two two-measure phrases or a single four-measure phrase which allows you to finger a new chord each measure but remain true to a G chord. The following active chords and progressions are designed to be used in your songs and playing whenever you have extended numbers of measures on the same chord. These active chords and progressions can also be great to use as a background for a solo and improvising when playing with other instrumentalists and vocalists. If you are playing songs that already contain many chords which change on a measure by measure basis (e.g. Nirvana, Pearl Jam, Hendrix, etc.), you may not need these new fingerings. Your musical material may be varied and interesting enough as written by the artists. However, the following chords will open new possibilities to you and your students.

I have included the notes of each chord on a treble clef above the chord charts. However, the note order does not match the pitches as played from the sixth through first strings of the guitar. The treble clef notes are there to help you relate what your fingers are doing to the music theory aspect of why a chord sounds like it does. You may use your existing repertoire of right-hand strums and arpeggios, or, you can combine these new chords with the "Vital Strums, Picks, and Plucks" outlined in Skills #12–15. Work at your own speed when learning. If you are acting as a music leader for others (including music therapist or educator), work at a speed which challenges your students, but which ensures their success. Some of the subskills may need to be broken down further for maximum student learning. You will find blank Teaching Outlines on pages vii and viii of this book for your use in this endeavor.

## Skill #1: Alternate G Chord and Superimposed Chords

I have started with this chord combination because it is one of the easiest to hip-start your playing. You are probably used to playing a G chord with your first, second, and third fingers. This is fine, but it leaves the left-hand pinkie with nothing to do. By using the second, third, and fourth left-hand fingers instead, you now have the first finger to play notes on the middle strings. The teaching outline shows four chords. The G chord is now newly-fingered, and allows for movement to the Am7/G (also sometimes called a C6/G), the A7/G, and a D7sus4/G. The /G means that a G note remains in the bass. This gives all the chords a common feel. You may play these four chords in sequence when you have extended hang time on a G chord. You may also substitute the Am7/G for a C chord when moving to or from a G. This will be reminiscent of John Denver's Sunshine *On My Shoulders* and Paul Simon songs such as *Me and Julio Down by the Schoolyard*. You will notice that the V7 chord (in this case a D7) remains suspended with a fourth in the treble and bass. This sound can be heard in the songs of many fine acoustic players such as James Taylor, David Wilcox, and Mary Chapin Carpenter. By not resolving to a plain old V7 chord, we keep some interest and movement. Not everything you play needs to be totally tidy—let some non-chord tones remain unresolved. This first teaching outline is simple on purpose to get you started with success. Try any strum you like, as long as the bottom G note is always played. Enjoy!

## Skill #2: D Chord with Moving Bass Patterns

D Major is a great chord to use for moving bass patterns. Skill #2 represents some of many possibilities. The progression in the top row has a bluesy sound due to the use of the lowered 7th, or C. The bottom row sounds a little more jazz/popish because of the raised or major 7th ($C^\sharp$). Chords used in progressions such as these have lent a classic sound to songs such as Neil Young's *Needle and the Damage Done* and the Beatles' *Dear Prudence*. Really accent the bass here. If you use your right-hand thumb to pluck the bass and then strum up and/or down with the other four right-hand fingers, you can create some nice effects. Adding a right-hand slap on beats two and four will create yet another level of interest (see Skills #12–15). Of course, finger picking is always an option. Use the thumb for the bass notes, and the index, middle and ring fingers for the top three strings. Notice that the dominant seventh chord (in this case an A7 chord) is left with a suspended fourth. Don't resolve this to a normal A7. This sounds more contemporary, and is a classic trademark of great acoustic players such as James Taylor, who immortalized this concept in early songs such as *Sweet Baby James* and *Fire and Rain*. You can use the chords in Skill #2 whenever you are hanging on a D Major chord and want to create some interest. The chords were diagrammed in an order that will permit you to play them from right to left in a circular pattern. Vary your rhythms, strums and arpeggios to create more interesting sounds. You can use these progressions to fill in between chord changes, and substitute them for more triad-based square progressions. Experiment with them and you will find some favorite uses of your own!

## Skill #3: G Chord with Moving Bass Patterns

These chords follow the same basic principal as Skill #2, but here we are working out of a G Major tonality. As in Skill #1, the chords can be played using a variety of right-hand techniques. You can also play them from left to right in sequence to create a nice circular progression. The top row has a bluesey sound due to the lowered seventh (note the suspended V7 chord), and the bottom row again sounds lighter and more in a jazz/pop realm. If you (or your students/clients) are feeling adventurous, play the chords in Skills #1 and 2 in order. This will give you a sixteen-measure progression which you can use as a base for improvisation. Notice how the D7sus at the end of Skill #1 will lead into the D Major chord at the start of Skill #2 in a very slippery sort of way.

# SKILL #1   Alternate G Chord and Superimposed Chords

Subskills:  I.  1
              II.  1 to 2 to 1 to 2
             III.  1 to 2 to 3 to 2
             IV.  1 to 2 to 3 to 4

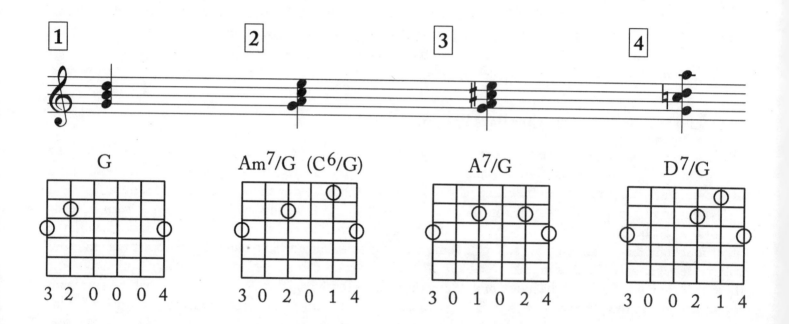

## PROGRESS DATA

| Date | | | | | | | | | | | |
|---|---|---|---|---|---|---|---|---|---|---|---|
| Subskill #(s) | | | | | | | | | | | |
| Prompt Level | | | | | | | | | | | |

| Date | | | | | | | | | | | |
|---|---|---|---|---|---|---|---|---|---|---|---|
| Subskill #(s) | | | | | | | | | | | |
| Prompt Level | | | | | | | | | | | |

Prompts:    I–Independent;  G–Gestural;  P–Physical;  M–Manipulative;  O–Subskill/Skill not performed.

# SKILL #2   D Chord with Moving Bass Patterns

Subskills:  I.  1 to 2 to 3 to 2
II.  1 to 2 to 3 to 4 (top row)
III.  5 to 6 to 7 to 8 (bottom row)
IV.  1 to 2 to 3 to 4 to 5 to 6 to 7 to 8 (both rows)

| 1 | 2 | 3 | 4 |
|---|---|---|---|
| D | C$^{6+9}$ | G$^{6+9}$/B | Gm$^{6+9}$/B$\flat$ |
| X (0)  0  1  3  2 | X  2  0  1  3  0 | X  1  0  2  3  0 | X  1  0  2  3  0 |

| 5 | 6 | 7 | 8 |
|---|---|---|---|
| D | Dmaj$^{7+9}$/C$\sharp$ | G$^{6+9}$/B | A$^{7}$sus$^{4}$ |
| X (0)  0  1  3  2 | (X)  4  0  1  3  0 | X  1  0  2  3  0 | (0)  0  1  0  3  0 |

## PROGRESS DATA

| Date | | | | | | | | | | | | |
|---|---|---|---|---|---|---|---|---|---|---|---|---|
| Subskill #(s) | | | | | | | | | | | | |
| Prompt Level | | | | | | | | | | | | |

| Date | | | | | | | | | | | | |
|---|---|---|---|---|---|---|---|---|---|---|---|---|
| Subskill #(s) | | | | | | | | | | | | |
| Prompt Level | | | | | | | | | | | | |

Prompts:      I–Independent;  G–Gestural;  P–Physical;  M–Manipulative;  O–Subskill/Skill not performed.

# SKILL #3   G Chord with Moving Bass Patterns

Subskills:   I.   1 to 2 to 3 to 2
II.   1 to 2 to 3 to 4 (top row)
III.   5 to 6 to 7 to 8 (bottom row)
IV.   1 to 2 to 3 to 4 to 5 to 6 to 7 to 8 (both rows)

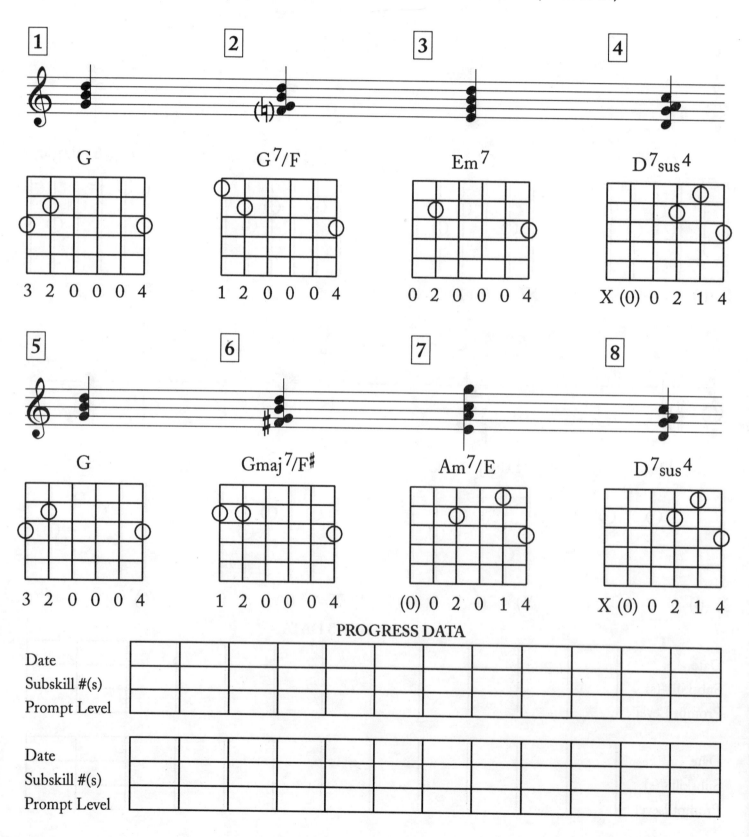

Prompts:      **I**–Independent;  **G**–Gestural;  **P**–Physical;  **M**–Manipulative;  **O**–Subskill/Skill not performed.

## Skill #4: C Chord with Moving Bass Patterns

As with Skills #2 and 3, these chords allow you to stay on a chord (here C Major) for a longer time without having the sound get dull and repetitive. You may use any right-hand techniques you wish as long as the bass notes are played. The top row again includes a lowered 7th for that blues sound. The bottom row descends more diatonically, and is reminiscent of Jerry Jeff Walker's immortal *Mr. Bojangles*. Playing all the chord boxes from left to right will bring you back to C Major over a course of eight measures. As always, we have substituted a dominant seventh chord with a suspended fourth for the more mundane V7 chord. If you are ready for a real challenge, play these eight chord boxes after those from Skills #2 and 3. You guessed it—we now have a 24 measure pattern. Feel free to change the chord order around to achieve new effects. Once you are used to fingering these new chords, you should be able to adapt easily to unfamiliar chord charts included in song books.

## Skill #5: A Chord with Moving Bass Patterns

This pattern is a little different. It relies on a combination of added non-chord tones, a diatonic major seventh, thumb movement, and a traditional E7 chord as a cadential pivot at the end of the progression. The four-chord sequence in the top four chord diagrams of the teaching outline works well when you are hanging on an A chord for an extended period. The final two chords are really meant to set up the return to the A chord. You could substitute an A7 for the Amaj7 for a bluesier sound. If you use a right-hand flatpick/string pluck technique and accent the bass notes with the flat pick, you can establish a nice Latin feel by playing the bass note on the down beat and then plucking up on the treble strings on the third and fourth beats (in common time) with a rest on the second beat. As always, you can follow all eight diagrams left to right for nifty eight bar patterns. You may also be creative and change or substitute chords for variations.

## Skill #6: E7 Moving (Blues) Chord Patterns and Progression

As you know, the blues sound is always a hip sound. There is something about that dominant seventh feel that makes for interesting and contemporary guitar work. The ongoing success of guitarists like Eric Clapton and Bonnie Raitt attests to that fact. We begin here with an E7 pattern and progression. It is labeled mixolydian because the seventh scale degree (D) is lowered, while the feeling is basically major (with a G$\sharp$ throughout). The chords begin innocently enough with an E7, but progress through a kind of turn-around. You can play the first two chords back and forth as a vamp on an E7 sound at first, and then progress to the first four chords in order. Notice that the fourth chord is a variant of a C7 chord (enharmonically equivalent to the raised 5 th in the key of E). Having this resolve back to the E7 chord sounds very hip. You may also play all eight chords in a row to form a nice eight-bar progression complete with a dominant seventh chord at the end! Try this with a flatpick/pluck (Skills #14 and 15) to really bring your playing to life. Remember that you can always add lead playing. Refer to *Beginning Rock Guitar for Music Leaders* for lead patterns that will work over an E7 chord.

## Skill #7: A7 Moving Mixolydian (Blues) Chord Patterns and Progression

As with Skill #6, we are exploring some blues sounds which use the mixolydian mode. Like E7, A7 works well because of the available open strings which are part of the tonalities. One different sound here is of a descending progression going from A7 to G6+9 to Fmaj7+9 to E7. The A7 to A resolution truly sounds mixolydian because of the lowered seventh, or G. The Fmaj7+9 really serves to set up the E7, as it approaches it chromatically by a half step. This altered F chord is, thus, a passing chord, making it truly active. As with other skill groups, you can play the top four chord boxes as a vamp over an A7 sound, or you can play all eight chord boxes in a row as a repeating progression. Use any strum, pick, or pick/pluck combination you like, as long as the bass notes are brought out.

# SKILL #4   C Chord with Moving Bass Patterns

Subskills:   I.   1 to 2 to 3 to 2
               II.   1 to 2 to 3 to 4 (top row)
             III.   5 to 6 to 7 to 8 (bottom row)
            IV.   1 to 2 to 3 to 4 to 5 to 6 to 7 to 8 (both rows)

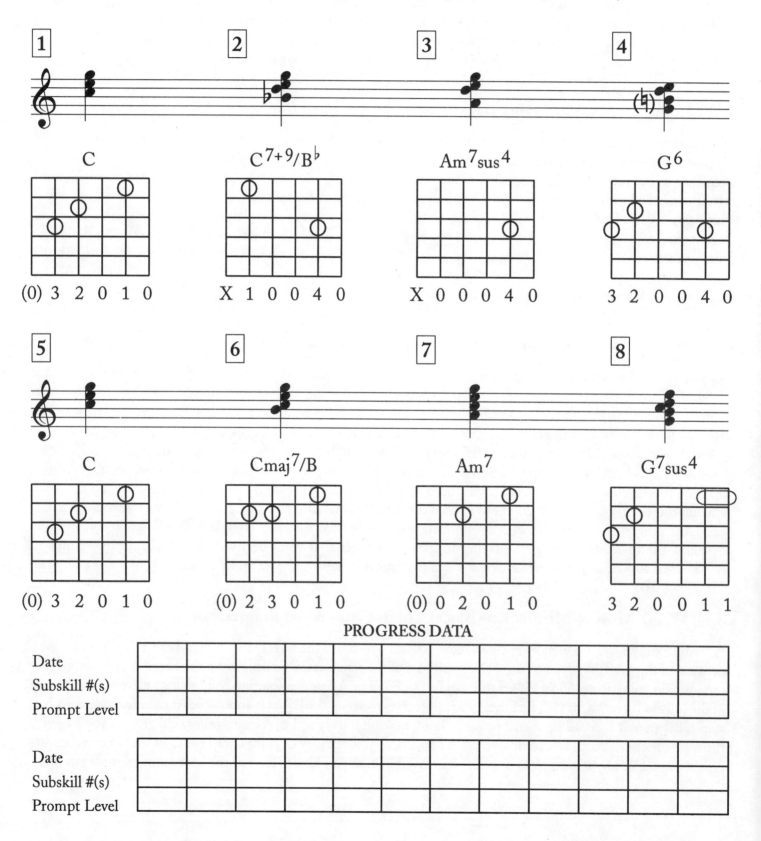

PROGRESS DATA

| Date | | | | | | | | | | | |
| --- | --- | --- | --- | --- | --- | --- | --- | --- | --- | --- | --- |
| Subskill #(s) | | | | | | | | | | | |
| Prompt Level | | | | | | | | | | | |

| Date | | | | | | | | | | | |
| --- | --- | --- | --- | --- | --- | --- | --- | --- | --- | --- | --- |
| Subskill #(s) | | | | | | | | | | | |
| Prompt Level | | | | | | | | | | | |

Prompts:      **I**–Independent;   **G**–Gestural;   **P**–Physical;   **M**–Manipulative;   **O**–Subskill/Skill not performed.

# SKILL #5 A Chord with Moving Bass Patterns

Subskills: I. 1 to 2 to 3 to 2
II. 1 to 2 to 3 to 4 (top row)
III. 5 to 6 to 7 to 8 (bottom row)
IV. 1 to 2 to 3 to 4 to 5 to 6 to 7 to 8 (both rows)

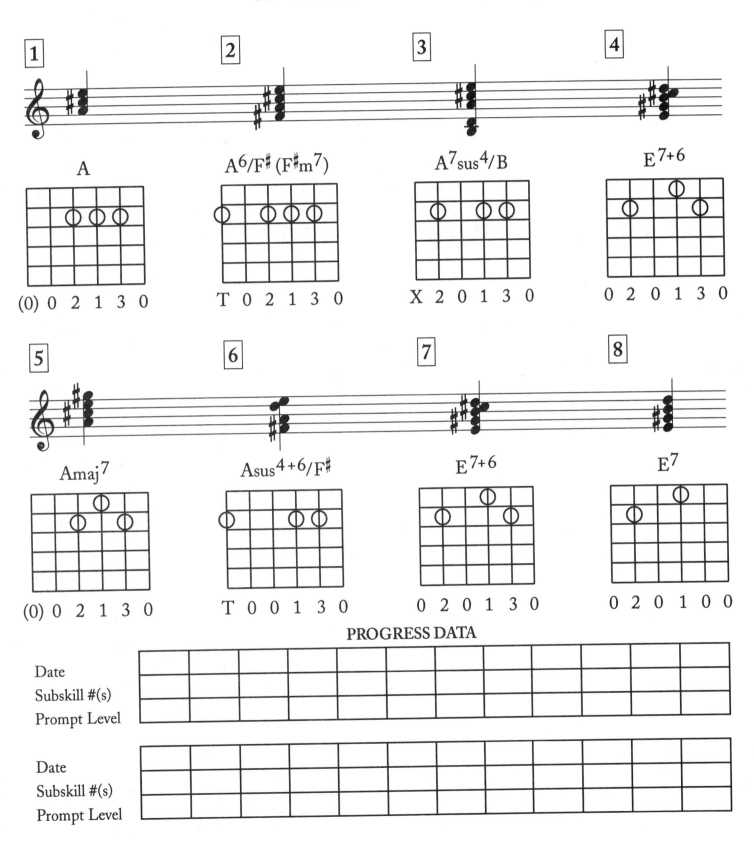

PROGRESS DATA

| Date | | | | | | | | | | |
|---|---|---|---|---|---|---|---|---|---|---|
| Subskill #(s) | | | | | | | | | | |
| Prompt Level | | | | | | | | | | |

| Date | | | | | | | | | | |
|---|---|---|---|---|---|---|---|---|---|---|
| Subskill #(s) | | | | | | | | | | |
| Prompt Level | | | | | | | | | | |

Prompts:  I–Independent;  G–Gestural;  P–Physical;  M–Manipulative;  O–Subskill/Skill not performed.

# SKILL #6   E$^7$ Moving Mixolydian Chord Patterns

Subskills:  I.  1 to 2 to 1 to 2

II.  1 to 2 to 3 to 4 (top row)

III.  5 to 6 to 7 to 8 (bottom row)

IV.  1 to 2 to 3 to 4 to 5 to 6 to 7 to 8 (both rows)

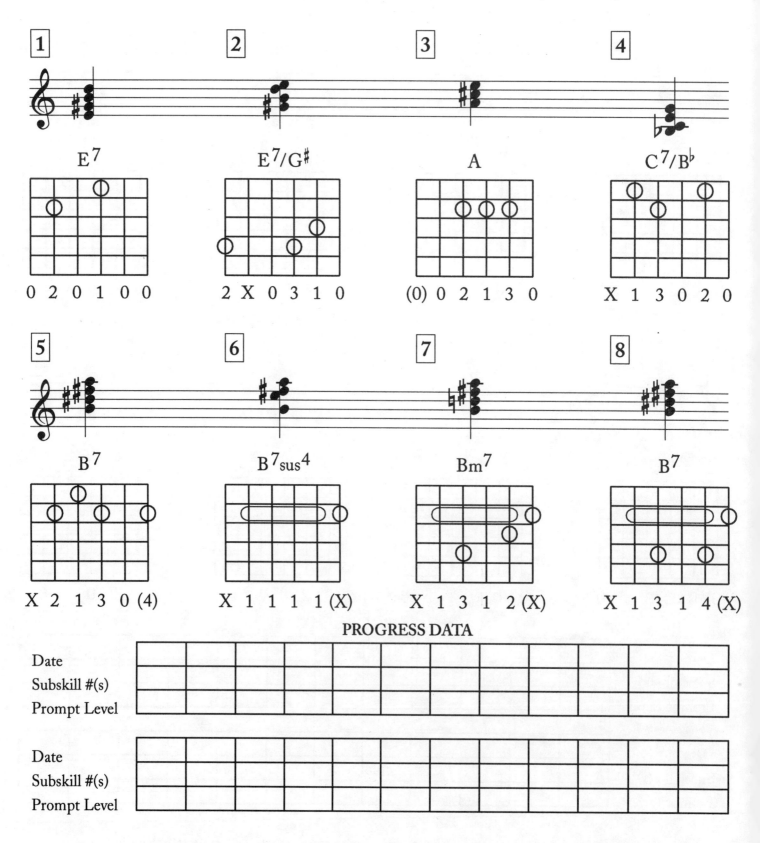

| 1 | 2 | 3 | 4 |
|---|---|---|---|
| E$^7$ | E$^7$/G$^\sharp$ | A | C$^7$/B$^\flat$ |
| 0 2 0 1 0 0 | 2 X 0 3 1 0 | (0) 0 2 1 3 0 | X 1 3 0 2 0 |

| 5 | 6 | 7 | 8 |
|---|---|---|---|
| B$^7$ | B$^7$sus$^4$ | Bm$^7$ | B$^7$ |
| X 2 1 3 0 (4) | X 1 1 1 1 (X) | X 1 3 1 2 (X) | X 1 3 1 4 (X) |

## PROGRESS DATA

| Date | | | | | | | | | | | | | |
|------|---|---|---|---|---|---|---|---|---|---|---|---|---|
| Subskill #(s) | | | | | | | | | | | | | |
| Prompt Level | | | | | | | | | | | | | |

| Date | | | | | | | | | | | | | |
|------|---|---|---|---|---|---|---|---|---|---|---|---|---|
| Subskill #(s) | | | | | | | | | | | | | |
| Prompt Level | | | | | | | | | | | | | |

Prompts:     **I**−Independent;  **G**−Gestural;  **P**−Physical;  **M**−Manipulative;  **O**−Subskill/Skill not performed.

# SKILL #7  A⁷ Moving Mixolydian Chord Patterns

Subskills:  I.  1 to 2 to 3 to 2
II.  1 to 2 to 3 to 4 (top row)
III.  5 to 6 to 7 to 8 (bottom row)
IV.  1 to 2 to 3 to 4 to 5 to 6 to 7 to 8 (both rows)

| 1 | 2 | 3 | 4 |
|---|---|---|---|
| $A^7$ | $A^7sus^4$ | $A^7$ | $A^7sus^{4+\natural 6}$ |
| (0)  0  2  0  3  0 | (0)  0  2  0  1  0 | (0)  0  2  0  3  0 | (0)  0  2  0  3  0 |

| 5 | 6 | 7 | 8 |
|---|---|---|---|
| $A^7$ | $G^{6+9}$ | $F maj^{7+9}$ | $E^7$ |
| (0)  0  2  0  3  0 | 2  0  0  0  3  0 | 2  0  0  0  3  0 | 0  2  0  1  0  0 |

## PROGRESS DATA

| Date | | | | | | | | | | | |
|---|---|---|---|---|---|---|---|---|---|---|---|
| Subskill #(s) | | | | | | | | | | | |
| Prompt Level | | | | | | | | | | | |

| Date | | | | | | | | | | | |
|---|---|---|---|---|---|---|---|---|---|---|---|
| Subskill #(s) | | | | | | | | | | | |
| Prompt Level | | | | | | | | | | | |

Prompts:  **I**–Independent;  **G**–Gestural;  **P**–Physical;  **M**–Manipulative;  **O**–Subskill/Skill not performed.

## Skill #8: D7 Moving Mixolydian (Blues) Chord Patterns and Progression

This progression starts out with a D7 chord. What follows is basically a harmonization of a D mixolydian scale with ascending chords. You will notice that three chords leave the B string open. This is done to make the upward progression easier, as the second three chords of the top row on the teaching outline only use two fingers. It also creates a nice suspended feeling, as that open B string creates an added sixth. The bottom row still uses only two fingers, but the top two or three strings are barred, increasing the difficulty level. Subskill #1 makes for a nice vamp off a D7 chord. Subskill #2 extends this upwards, but can still loop back to a D7 chord. Subskill #3 completes the full cycle. You may notice that several chords have the same names but are fingered differently. For this reason, the chords have been numbered for easier identification. As always, you may wish to create your own variation and write it out on a blank teaching outline for you or your student. For a strum or arpeggio pattern, try a shuffle feeling. You may wish to contrast this with straight eighth notes as a variation. Just make sure to keep the open D string in the bass to emphasize the D feeling.

## Skill #9: G7 Moving Mixolydian (Blues) Chord Patterns and Progression

This progression is based out of G mixolydian. You may use either two-finger chords which utilize left-hand fingers on the bass strings and the second string, or three-finger chords which add the first string. Note that the first two chords involve muting the fifth string as the second finger depresses the bottom string. This is not difficult, just let that second finger lay a little flatter than usual over the fifth string. As with previous chord combinations, the first two chords in sequence can form a bluesy-sounding vamp over a G chord because of the lowered seventh (F) You can combine the first four chords in sequence, and finally all eight to create a nice progression. Note that the progression ends with a A7 sus 4 chord, which could lead to a D chord progression (see Skill #8). You could also lead into the above chords from Skill #8. In fact, you could play all our multi-measure skills in a row for a rather complex progression! Mix and match progressions as you like, and let your ear be the guide.

# SKILL #8 D⁷ Moving Mixolydian Chord Patterns

Subskills:   I.   1 to 2 to 3 to 2
II.   1 to 2 to 3 to 4 (top row)
III.   5 to 6 to 7 to 8 (bottom row)
IV.   1 to 2 to 3 to 4 to 5 to 6 to 7 to 8 (both rows)

| 1 | 2 | 3 | 4 |

$D^7$          G/D          $D^{7+6}$(no 3)          G/D ($D^{5+6}$)

X (0) 0 2 1 3          X (0) 0 2 0 1          X (0) 0 2 0 3          X (0) 0 2 0 3

| 5 | 6 | 7 | 8 |

C/D          Bm/D          Am/D          G/D

X (0) 0 2 1 1          X (0) 0 1 1 1          X (0) 0 1 1 1          X (0) 0 2 1 1

## PROGRESS DATA

| | | | | | | | | | | | |
|---|---|---|---|---|---|---|---|---|---|---|---|
| Date | | | | | | | | | | | |
| Subskill #(s) | | | | | | | | | | | |
| Prompt Level | | | | | | | | | | | |

| | | | | | | | | | | | |
|---|---|---|---|---|---|---|---|---|---|---|---|
| Date | | | | | | | | | | | |
| Subskill #(s) | | | | | | | | | | | |
| Prompt Level | | | | | | | | | | | |

Prompts:     I–Independent;  G–Gestural;  P–Physical;  M–Manipulative;  O–Subskill/Skill not performed.

# SKILL #9   $G^7$ Moving Mixolydian Chord Patterns

Subskills:  I.  1 to 2 to 1 to 2
II.  1 to 2 to 3 to 4 (top row)
III.  5 to 6 to 7 to 8 (bottom row)
IV.  1 to 2 to 3 to 4 to 5 to 6 to 7 to 8 (both rows)

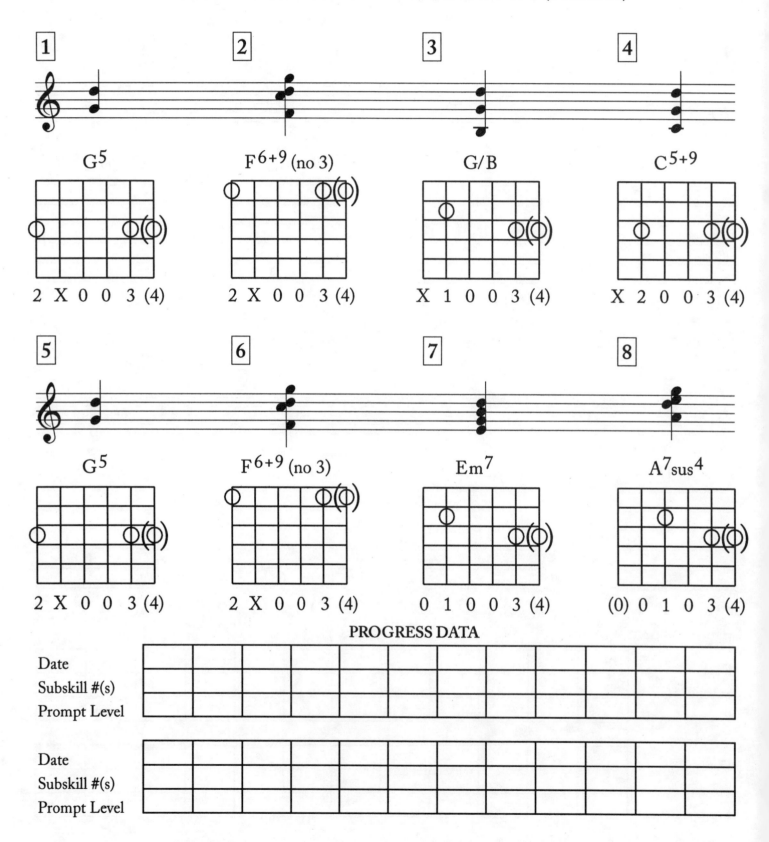

PROGRESS DATA

| Date | | | | | | | | | | | |
|---|---|---|---|---|---|---|---|---|---|---|---|
| Subskill #(s) | | | | | | | | | | | |
| Prompt Level | | | | | | | | | | | |

| Date | | | | | | | | | | | |
|---|---|---|---|---|---|---|---|---|---|---|---|
| Subskill #(s) | | | | | | | | | | | |
| Prompt Level | | | | | | | | | | | |

Prompts:      **I**−Independent;  **G**−Gestural;  **P**−Physical;  **M**−Manipulative;  **O**−Subskill/Skill not performed.

## Skill #10: E minor Moving Chord Patterns and Progression

The key of E minor is great to work out of because of the open strings. The first, second, third, and sixth strings are all members of the E minor triad, and the fourth string is the seventh of the chord. In order to stretch your sonorous sounds a little, I have written a pattern that uses no garden-variety E minor chords (except for the optional ending in the last chord chart). Notice, the second finger of the left-hand always remains on the fifth string second fret, thus providing an anchor for the moving chords. As in previous progressions, the top row of chords has been written to be played as a repeating loop during any span of measures which uses an e minor chord in a song. The first two subskills involve chords in the top row of chord charts. Subskill #3 expands the progression to include the first two chords of the second chart row. The total progression of eight chords resolves with a B7 chord. However, you may end with a plain E minor chord. Because I have written an Em7 chord with two different fingerings, I have numbered the chord charts. This is a fun progression, and can be played with many rhythmic strums, including those with a Latin feel.

## Skill #11: A minor Moving Chord Patterns and Progression

Like the pleasures of an E minor progression, a minor makes use of open strings, including the top and bottom E strings and the fifth string (open A.) We also include the open G string here, as this brings in the diatonically lowered seventh, a very nice, soft sound when combined with other chord extensions and non-chord tones. This progression is quite different, however, from previous examples; it includes more chords and chord qualities (major and minor sonorities.) What keeps the progression together is the use of the open A string as a drone or pedal point. Like the previous progression, the first subskill involves a vamp over the tonic chord, here an A minor chord. Notice how the seventh slips from a raised seventh to the diatonic seventh and back up a half step. This four-chord combination sounds like an early version of a James Bond theme or an acoustic *Secret Agent Man.* Though there are a couple of passing chords that sound rather odd out of context, they prick up the ears in context, adding interest. These are found in the bottom row of chord charts.

We have now come to the end of the active chords section of the book. There are so many more possibilities, but I think you should now be used to looking at chord possibilities in new ways. You may take Skills #1–11 and transfer them to new material. Remember also that guitar learning is truly a lifelong process. Consider the skills that we have covered as one small part of that process. We will now look at some contemporary right-hand techniques to complement Skills #1–11.

# SKILL #10   E minor Moving Chord Patterns

Subskills:  I.  1 to 2 to 3 to 2
II.  1 to 2 to 3 to 4 (top row)
III.  1 to 2 to 3 to 4 to 5 to 6 (both rows)
IV.  1 to 2 to 3 to 4 to 5 to 6 to 7 to 8 (both rows)

| 1 | 2 | 3 | 4 |
|---|---|---|---|
| $Em^{7+9}$ | $Em^7$ | $Em^{7+\sharp6}$ | $Em^{7+6}$ |
| 0 2 0 0 0 3 | 0 2 0 0 4 0 | 0 2 0 0 3 0 | 0 2 0 0 1 0 |

| 5 | 6 | 7 | 8 |
|---|---|---|---|
| $Em^7$ | $Em^7sus^4$ (no 3) | $B^7sus^4/E$ | $B^7/E$ |
| 0 2 0 0 0 0 | 0 2 0 3 0 0 | 0 2 1 3 0 0 | 0 2 1 3 0 4 |

## PROGRESS DATA

| Date |  |  |  |  |  |  |  |  |  |  |  |
|---|---|---|---|---|---|---|---|---|---|---|---|
| Subskill #(s) |  |  |  |  |  |  |  |  |  |  |  |
| Prompt Level |  |  |  |  |  |  |  |  |  |  |  |

| Date |  |  |  |  |  |  |  |  |  |  |  |
|---|---|---|---|---|---|---|---|---|---|---|---|
| Subskill #(s) |  |  |  |  |  |  |  |  |  |  |  |
| Prompt Level |  |  |  |  |  |  |  |  |  |  |  |

Prompts:     **I**–Independent;  **G**–Gestural;  **P**–Physical;  **M**–Manipulative;  **O**–Subskill/Skill not performed.

# SKILL #11  A minor Moving Chord Patterns

Subskills:  I.  1 to 2 to 3 to 2
II.  1 to 2 to 3 to 4 (top row)
III.  5 to 6 to 7 to 8 (bottom row)
IV.  1 to 2 to 3 to 4 to 5 to 6 to 7 to 8 (both rows)

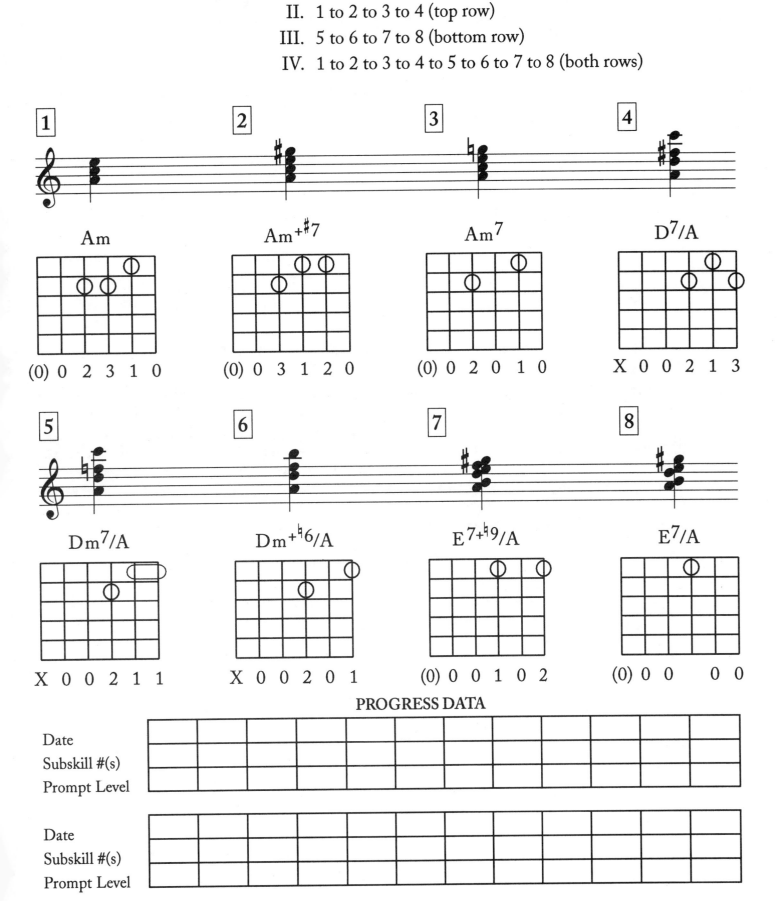

PROGRESS DATA

| Date | | | | | | | | | | | | |
|---|---|---|---|---|---|---|---|---|---|---|---|---|
| Subskill #(s) | | | | | | | | | | | | |
| Prompt Level | | | | | | | | | | | | |

| Date | | | | | | | | | | | | |
|---|---|---|---|---|---|---|---|---|---|---|---|---|
| Subskill #(s) | | | | | | | | | | | | |
| Prompt Level | | | | | | | | | | | | |

Prompts:    **I**–Independent;  **G**–Gestural;  **P**–Physical;  **M**–Manipulative;  **O**–Subskill/Skill not performed.

# SKILLS #12–15: VITAL STRUMS, PICKS, AND PLUCKS

The following skills are designed to produce a more rhythmic and interesting sound. They work well in any situation and bring new skills such as our active chords to life. The idea is to get away from traditional strumming and finger picking and make your playing sound fresh. These skills may be a challenge for you and your learners, but are worth it in the long run, as they can be applied to many different music playing situations.

## Skill #12: Rhythmic Strum with Right-Hand Damping

What we are doing here is building a simple to complex strumming pattern using rests as important parts of the rhythmic pattern. I have chosen a G chord, as this was the first active chord you learned. To keep the strings from ringing during the rests, we use the heel of the right-hand to quit or damp the strings. Practice Subskill #1 slowly, strumming across the strings and then laying the heel of the right-hand on the strings above the sound hole on the second beat of the pattern. Try to do this as smoothly as possible so that the damp/rest falls exactly on that second beat. This will take some practice. When Subskill #1 feels comfortable, move on to the nest subskill, this time adding a down-up strum on beat three. Progress through the subskills until you are playing the last example, a syncopated strum, with the eighth note rests falling at crucial points in the measure. You might want to combine subskills in order to create multi-measure patterns. Apply this skill to any of the active chords and progressions learned earlier in the book.

## Skill #13: Rhythmic Strum with Right-Hand Slapping

This skill extends what was learned in Skill #12 by using the right-hand to slap the strings above the sound hole instead of merely damping them. To get a really rhythmic sound, hit the strings with your flatpick as you slap. This slapping will seem awkward at first, but you will find it becomes part of your right-hand habits after you learn it. Remember to slap the strings hard enough to produce an audible sound. I nave notated the skill using a slash symbol (/) to indicate the slap, as it is not a sound and not a rest. Skill #3 used the second chord from Skill #1, the Am7 or C/G chord. In this way, you can combine Skills #12 and 13 in order to produce a chord change vamp that utilizes both of your new strumming techniques. As with Skill #12, the subskills add more rhythmic interest and challenge, while keeping the same basic technique. I hope you like this slapping skill, because we will soon be combining it with a picking/plucking combination (see Skill #15 for the *coup de grace*.)

# SKILL #12  Rhythmic Strum with Right-Hand Damping

Subskills:  I.   Quarter-note strum/damp
            II.  Quarter/eighth-note strum/damp
            III. Eighth-note strum/damp
            IV.  Syncopated eighth-note strum/damp

Skill Notation:  Alternate G chord (see Skill #1)        Strum:  D = down   U = up    dp = damp

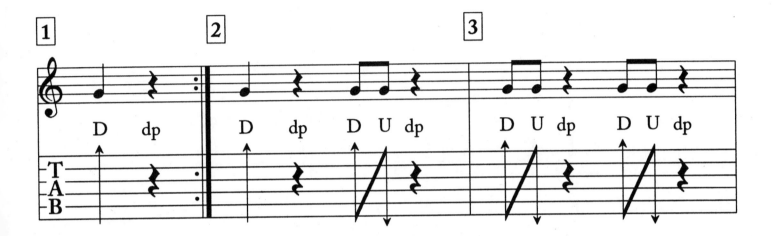

## PROGRESS DATA

| Date | | | | | | | | | | | | |
|---|---|---|---|---|---|---|---|---|---|---|---|---|
| Subskill #(s) | | | | | | | | | | | | |
| Prompt Level | | | | | | | | | | | | |

| Date | | | | | | | | | | | | |
|---|---|---|---|---|---|---|---|---|---|---|---|---|
| Subskill #(s) | | | | | | | | | | | | |
| Prompt Level | | | | | | | | | | | | |

Prompts:     I—Independent;  G—Gestural;  P—Physical;  M—Manipulative;  O—Subskill/Skill not performed.

# SKILL #13 Rhythmic Strum with Right-Hand Slap

Subskills:  I.  Quarter-note strum/slap
II.  Quarter/eighth-note strum/slap
III.  Eighth-note strum/slap
IV.  Syncopated eighth-note strum/slap

Skill Notation:  a min$^7$/G (see Skill #1)                    Strum:  D = down    U = up    S = slap

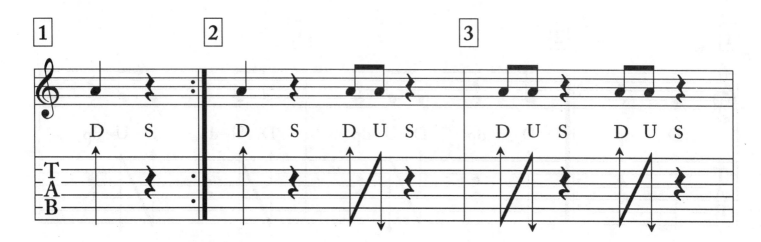

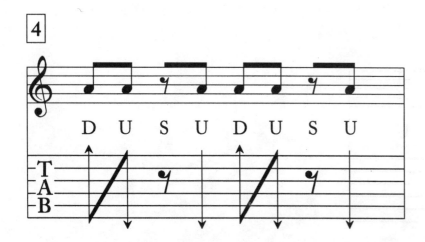

**PROGRESS DATA**

| Date | | | | | | | | | | | |
|---|---|---|---|---|---|---|---|---|---|---|---|
| Subskill #(s) | | | | | | | | | | | |
| Prompt Level | | | | | | | | | | | |

| Date | | | | | | | | | | | |
|---|---|---|---|---|---|---|---|---|---|---|---|
| Subskill #(s) | | | | | | | | | | | |
| Prompt Level | | | | | | | | | | | |

Prompts:     **I**–Independent;  **G**–Gestural;  **P**–Physical;  **M**–Manipulative;  **O**–Subskill/Skill not performed.

## Skill #14: Flat Picking with Right-Hand Plucking

I have put Skills #14 and 15 at the end, as they are potentially the most difficult. However, the end result is certainly worth the work along the way. The basic idea is to combine the techniques of flat picking and string plucking. Flat picking allows you to aggressively hit the bass strings, and plucking allows you to play the treble strings with an upward motion of the remaining three right-hand fingers. This technique has been used on many hit songs, including *Tears in Heaven* by Eric Clapton, *More Than Words* by Extreme, and many others. With this technique, you don't have to put the pick down every time you want to use your fingers to pluck strings. For example, you could use this concept to play *Stairway to Heaven* by Led Zeppelin. This classic song uses an acoustic guitar intro which is arpeggiated, but later goes into a heavier strum using a pick. Jimmy Page did both, so why shouldn't we! I have used a simple chord combination of a D5 (no third) and a C5 with an added 9 for interest. Notice that we are using only the third and fourth fingers (middle and ring) of the right hand for the plucking. Engaging the pinkie of the right hand is great, but takes a long time to develop. Feel free to add it as you gain dexterity with this concept. Remember to accent the bass string with the pick.

## Skill #15: Flat Picking with Right-Hand Plucking and Slapping

For our grand finale I have used some chords from Skill #9, specifically because the top treble string is optional and the bass is prominent. We are now combining elements of the slapping technique with the picking and plucking. Remember that this is only one possibility for combining skills. You will encounter similar techniques in guitar tab books and magazines. You may also choose to arrange music to make use of the techniques involved in Skill #15. Be brave and don't worry about mistakes on the way. Remember that the flat pick will play the bass parts and the middle and ring fingers will pluck up on the chord notes.

That rounds out our fifteen skills. I hope that you and your students have picked up some new and exciting sounds along the way. Please adapt these skills as you see fit, and try applying them to various music styles and compositions. Remember that your playing should reflect your individuality—so don't worry about playing exactly like everyone else. Good luck, we'll see you in the pages of our next guitar book!

# SKILL #14  Flat Picking with Right-Hand Plucking

Subskills:   I.  Pick/pluck $D^5$
             II.  Pick/pluck $D^5/C^5$ add 9
             III.  Syncopated $D^5$ pick/pluck to $C^5$ pick/pluck
             IV.  Syncopated $D^5$ pick/pluck to syncopated $C^5$ add 9 pick/pluck

Skill Notation: $D^5$

Strum:  pkD = pick down    plU = pluck up

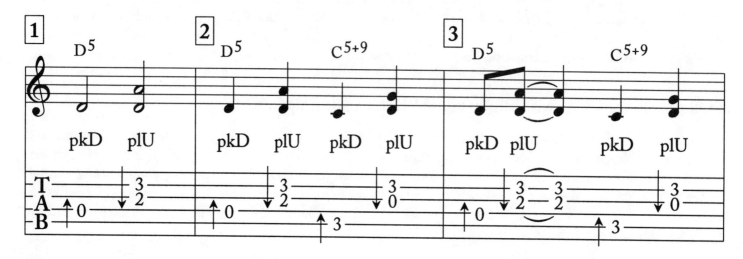

## PROGRESS DATA

| Date | | | | | | | | | | | |
|---|---|---|---|---|---|---|---|---|---|---|---|
| Subskill #(s) | | | | | | | | | | | |
| Prompt Level | | | | | | | | | | | |

| Date | | | | | | | | | | | |
|---|---|---|---|---|---|---|---|---|---|---|---|
| Subskill #(s) | | | | | | | | | | | |
| Prompt Level | | | | | | | | | | | |

Prompts:     **I**−Independent;  **G**−Gestural;  **P**−Physical;  **M**−Manipulative;  **O**−Subskill/Skill not performed.

# SKILL #15   Flat Picking with Right-Hand Plucking
## Slapping & Damping

Subskills:  I.  Pick, pluck, slap, damp (rest)
II.  Syncopated pick, pluck, pick, slap
III.  Syncopated pick, pluck, pick, slap, pick
IV.  Syncopated pick, pluck, pick, slap, pluck

Skill Notation: G⁵ chord                    Strum:  pkD = pick down   plU = pluck up   S = slap   dp = damp (rest)

## PROGRESS DATA

| Date | | | | | | | | | | |
|---|---|---|---|---|---|---|---|---|---|---|
| Subskill #(s) | | | | | | | | | | |
| Prompt Level | | | | | | | | | | |

| Date | | | | | | | | | | |
|---|---|---|---|---|---|---|---|---|---|---|
| Subskill #(s) | | | | | | | | | | |
| Prompt Level | | | | | | | | | | |

Prompts:     I–Independent;  G–Gestural;  P–Physical;  M–Manipulative;  O–Subskill/Skill not performed.